PREFACE

The secret of a good sermon is to have a good beginning and a good ending; and to have the two as close together as possible.

---- *George Burns*

After many years of experience as a Program Manager, I have decided to write a small book on the large topic of leading winning project teams. Since I believe Mr Burns' advice should also apply to business sermons, it is a small book.

I will skip a summary of my many relevant experiences and assume they are exaggerated elsewhere. I am not writing this book for management theorists but for Program Managers, for people who have to lead teams, meet challenges, and achieve business results in the real world. Today's tough business environment makes this book's practical actions even more important.

I am convinced that the main points of this book are universal and can be of practical use, with little or no adjustment, on your program. I invite and encourage your skepticism. As Mark Twain is reported to have said: "Be careful

1

about reading health books. You may die of a misprint." A similar caution is appropriate when reading business books, including this one. Blindly adopting their recommendations might, at the very least, make your program very ill.

For those who enjoy stories about looking for cheese or the spacing dynamics of boy scouts marching through the woods, there will be some disappointment. I assume you are too busy leading to read long tales written by amateur storywriters, and would prefer an author who gets quickly to the point. To that end, each Chapter title is a main point, a recommendation. You will not have to mine this book and sift it carefully for valuable ore. There are no pictures or cartoons, only straight talk.

Finally, this book does not address what I'll call the science of program management. It does not describe those fundamental practices and related management systems that allow you to define and measure and manage the many cost, schedule, technical, configuration, performance and other baselines that are essential to program success. Simply stated, your program and your people will not succeed if you are not fully immersed in these operational details. You can't lead your team to success from some faraway tower with your fingernails spotlessly clean.

However, beyond all these necessary fundamentals, beyond all the science of program execution, there is some art to program management and leading winning teams and that art is the focus of this book.

CHAPTER ONE: DEFINE THE DESTINATION AND ALWAYS KEEP IT IN SIGHT

It seems pretty obvious but it's truly amazing how many teams don't achieve this fundamental need to define the destination. It's critically important that your program team understands, and is able to describe, where the team is going. What are you trying to accomplish? What's the program's overall purpose? I believe this destination description shouldn't be too abstract. It needs to be tangible: the team needs to know what it will look and feel like once you are there.

For a larger program team, most members must have this shared understanding, this destination fluency. For smaller teams, it's essential that everyone truly get it. I don't care if you call it a Destination or Vision or Mission Statement or even something else as long as there's a shared appreciation of what the team is seeking to accomplish over the longer term. This is not a high school poetry class and team members do not need to be asked to recite a finely crafted destination description word for word, but they need to be able to articulate the Vision in a way that is meaningful to them.

Who establishes this program Vision? I really don't think it makes much difference if the Program Manager consults only himself (or herself, of course) and then simply proclaims the Vision or if the entire team for a smaller program, or small cadre from a larger team, debates for weeks before arriving at the consensus result. However, since the Vision needs to be fully embraced if it's going to energize the team, more participative approaches make some sense. I have seen both approaches work well.

What is more essential is that the Program Manger or business leader is deeply immersed in this destination-defining process. You can't delegate this to a "Vision Champion" and then be absent until it's time to drop by and select among some options. I have seen this approach and it doesn't work.

On one occasion, my Division General Manager, fully recognizing the survival imperative to transform his business, asked me, his Business Development executive, to *lead* this change effort. I told him I would gladly *facilitate* this important effort but that he needed to be personally and fully engaged. He had to lead the transformation and to be its clear Champion. Although the GM nodded his agreement, he instead remained very focused on the crisis of the week and the financials for the current quarter, and he did not invest his time and energy in this effort as one of his priorities. As a result, people did not believe there was an urgent need to change and no real transformation occurred. As a side note, when you are newly assigned to lead a program, one of your first tasks should be to determine if a clear destination description already exists. If not, achieving this shared definition needs to be a priority. If there is an existing statement, you need to review it with your team and ensure you fully understand it. Then, you can either accept it or *lead* the effort to develop an alternative picture of the future. You need to be very objective in making this assessment. Although it might be tempting to change or replace the Vision just to "make your mark," you need to hold your ego in check on this one. The Vision already in place might be fine and, if so, you should embrace it and make your mark elsewhere.

Of course, a related priority task is to determine if the destination statement has been fully communicated to and embraced by the team. Has it been kept in sight or is it just a nice graphic buried deep in the Program Plan?

Earlier, I stated that the Vision should not be abstract. The destination, and the path to reaching it, should be tangible and measurable. After all, the team needs to know if it is making, or not making, progress and it surely need to know when it has arrived at the destination. Of course, your program Vision also needs to be fully aligned and supportive of the Vision for the larger enterprise.

Importantly, the Vision must describe a destination that is worth reaching and one that is reasonably achievable. These qualities go hand in hand. If the effort is truly worthwhile, it must represent some level of challenge, with an associated risk of failure. If it's a piece of cake to achieve the Vision, it's not worthwhile and will not energize your team. If it's unreasonable (a risk of failure approaching 100%), it will also fail to energize your people.

It's absolutely amazing how hard teams will work to achieve the greatest challenges and how little energy they will invest to achieve challenges that are simply outrageous. Obviously, there is some subjectivity here and what may seem an unreasonable goal to me may seem quite reasonable to you. However, beyond the range of such individual perspectives are goals that *any* rational, prudent person would judge unachievable. Amazingly, I have worked for business leaders who routinely challenged their teams to achieve such fantastic goals, knowing full well they could not be met. One GM would take any schedule-to-go estimate and reduce it by at least 50%, sometimes more. His philosophy was that people worked just hard enough to achieve whatever schedule milestone was on the table; therefore, since any established milestone was essentially a not-earlier-than date, one might as well make it as early as possible. Once, when I pushed back on one of his outrageous schedule challenges, he asked me if I scratched my head until it bled thinking about how to meet his accelerated milestones. When I replied "no," he forcefully told me that was his expectation.

To the extent that people tried in good faith to meet his unreasonable milestones, they often adopted shortcuts that led to a host of quality and product integrity issues. However, most people just disengaged from the challenge altogether since there was no way, no matter how much your head bled, to meet the schedule goals. And, of course, many people just played the game by dramatically padding their schedule-to-go projections. This may have been the culture the GM grew up in and could explain in part why he had such a cut-every-estimate-in-half philosophy in the first place. However, a business culture that doesn't *keep it real* and actually encourages such game playing is a disaster waiting to happen.

When I managed a military aircraft program, one that was nearing the end of its product cycle, our Vision was quite straightforward: we simply aspired to extend the production line for at least a decade. The destination was literally a sight picture for the team. Even if you had retired or moved on, you could visit the plant ten years in the future. If you saw new build aircraft coming off the production line and being accepted by a customer, you knew the Vision destination had been reached. This simple Vision drove many, many actions. The team had to assure our aircraft product remained affordable and relevant to our customers and these imperatives informed our investment decisions. The team had to identify potential customers, both existing and new, who were likely to purchase our product in the near term; again, this drove our investments into selected sales campaigns.

Finally, the Vision, and its many implications must be relentlessly communicated if you are to keep the destination in sight and the team engaged. This is especially challenging for larger program teams, for those with members, including suppliers, who work at multiple sites, and for those that rely significantly on "functional support."

Once you have a clear, tangible destination, you will need a top level Roadmap, one that describes the path from today to the future state you and your team have committed to reach.

CHAPTER TWO: DEVELOP A
ROADMAP TO YOUR DESTINATION

Now that your program has dealt with *that Vision thing*, and team members can articulate the destination they are collectively committed to reach, the real work can begin. How is the team going to get there?

Again, this course or Roadmap can be defined by you, the Program Manager, or it can be a collective effort by the team. Unlike the Vision definition effort, where I am somewhat ambivalent about the best approach, I strongly recommend that Roadmap development be the result of a collaborative team effort. The reason is simple. I am convinced this team approach will result in a superior how-do-we-get-there plan. Also, by engaging the team in charting the course, they will naturally feel even more accountable for executing the Roadmap plan and reaching the destination.

In Chapter One, I briefly described a program Vision example that painted a sight picture of new build aircraft being delivered ten years in the future. Let's assume that a current backlog of forty-eight aircraft only drives deliveries for four years at a notional production rate of about twelve aircraft per year. To achieve the Vision, the team needs to capture orders for an additional six years or seventy-two aircraft (6 years x 12 aircraft per year = 72 aircraft). In addition, assuming the cycle time from contract order to aircraft delivery is three years, the team needs a new aircraft order within the next year. If that near-term order is for just twenty-four aircraft, an additional order is needed within the following two years, since any break in production, with the attendant loss of experienced production workers, would require a prohibitively expensive production line restart. The math is straightforward and the challenge of achieving the Vision is becoming clear.

In this example, the Roadmap, at a top level, must identify the key aircraft sales opportunities, their timing, and the investments required. These selected sales campaigns are the result of a candid, *don't-kid-yourself* analysis of the marketplace that assesses how likely it is that a given customer, a foreign government in this example, will actually budget for and then conduct an aircraft competition (Pgo). The analysis also looks at the anticipated aircraft requirements, the probable competitors and evaluates how likely it is that your aircraft is ultimately selected (Pwin). This is no place for wishful thinking.

The Roadmap must include detailed plans for improving the execution of current production contracts as well. A highly satisfied customer is often a future buyer. In any case, a reputation for the on-time delivery of a quality product that meets or exceeds customer expectations is a tremendous market discriminator. The Roadmap, at lower levels of detail, also must identify the specific investments needed to lower costs since the product not only has to remain affordable in the marketplace but also must be sufficiently profitable to the larger enterprise to justify the required investments. Again, clear-eyed and intellectually honest financial analysis is needed to assess whether there's a reasonable and timely return on these affordability investments.

The use of metrics needs to be pervasive. The team needs to know if it is on or off the charted course. In this example, at the Roadmap's top level, the metrics need to track progress towards achieving a sale to Customer A in 20XX. Has the buying government approved a budget that supports a contract award in 20XX? Is the buying air force meeting their schedule for defining the top-level system requirements based on their desired operational capabilities and for releasing the solicitation document?

These are tangible, measurable benchmarks that tell you whether you or not you are on track. If not on track for a 20XX award, the team needs to take action. The details of the Roadmap will need to change while the ten-year destination remains fixed.

For example, perhaps there is a Customer B you are also tracking who is moving forward more aggressively and could possibly pull its planned award date forward to 20XX? Maybe there need to be new actions that focus resources and attention on this alternative? Perhaps the team needs to extend the current production deliveries by a few months to close the possible production delivery gap caused by Customer A's anticipated delay? Maybe the enterprise, if it considers your product to be in an excellent competitive position and has confidence the delay in Customer A's selection process will only be a few months, is willing to put company funds at risk and initiate the build cycle by placing orders for long lead material with selected suppliers? Again, a lot of analysis and objective, *don't-kid-yourself* analysis is required. In any case, the Roadmap is not fixed and is guaranteed to change as your team adapts to the dynamics of a marketplace in the real world. The good news is that there are many paths to your destination. You and your team need to anticipate and identify these contingent routes in advance and keep them viable if needed. As a veteran manager once told me: "Even a dumb bunny has more than one hole."

At more granular, lower levels of the Roadmap, the metrics involved increase dramatically. The team needs to measure *everything that's important,* especially those things that are leading indicators of problems yet to come. Don't be trapped into measuring lots and lots of things just because the data are easy to collect or because people have collected and reported these data for a long time. The team can lose focus on the truly important metrics if there is too much metric clutter.

A word of caution: as I said at the outset, developing Roadmaps or plans of any kind are real work. As the Program Manager, you need to insist that this hard work gets done. If you don't, your team will most likely create inadequate, lip-service-only plans which are not well thought out or even fully actionable. As the leader, you need to insist that not just the program Vision, but all goals, objectives, commitments, recovery efforts etc have a credible, actionable plan with clear accountability.

I have sometimes been asked whether I would rather have a great plan or great people. This is really a false choice since you need both. However, if you have great people, I am very confident they will create, with your leadership, a great plan.

CHAPTER THREE: NEVER FORGET-IT'S ALL ABOUT YOUR PEOPLE

Nothing is more important to the success of your program than the quality of the people on your team. Nothing! Their professional competence, talent, energy and integrity will determine success. It's not about creating the perfect organizational construct or team charters or even creating world class plans. Ultimately, you need to attract, develop and keep the very best people you can. With their hearts and brains engaged in achieving the program Vision, your team will almost certainly succeed.

Attracting Them

Why does anyone want to be on _your_ program? Perhaps they worked with you before, enjoyed the experience, and want more? Maybe the position being offered represents a promotion or a logical career move? Perhaps they are excited about the advanced technology your program seeks to create or to introduce in the marketplace? Maybe they are passionate about your product? Of course, a list of possible motivations could go on and on. You may or may not have a program that's particularly exciting. You may or may not have lots of positions with high grade and salary levels. But worst of all, your program may not have a widespread reputation for providing an environment that makes people feel trusted and respected. This is the critical factor and it is one you largely determine.

As the Program Manager, you need to create, nourish and advertise such an open culture. The next chapter focuses on how to meet this challenge. I believe this is the most important thing you can do to attract talent. You also need to ensure you have the appropriate grade levels for the jobs on your program; and you need to sell people on the challenge and excitement of achieving the program Vision. If you do these things, many people will want to be on your program team. Yes, if you build it, they will come. Your challenge will be to select the right people from among those many qualified candidates.

Interviews are hard. It's not easy to make the right choice, especially if the candidate pool includes many people you and your team do not already know. Technical competence may be relatively easy to determine, but important attributes like judgment, loyalty, integrity and energy are often hard to get a handle on during a brief interview session.

Some candidates are great interviewers and can provide wonderful, sometimes quite fanciful, answers to your questions. In one interview, I asked a candidate from another site whom I did not know to recall a specific experience in which he had implemented a recommendation from someone junior on his team. We heard a wonderful story of how he had encouraged the problem solution views of a shy, young member of his team; how he was not initially in agreement with those views; how he nonetheless listened carefully to the junior teammate's rationale and was ultimately persuaded to follow his recommendation. It was a great example of the value of diversity, active listening, and empowerment.

During my follow-up, I talked with a few people at the candidate's home site who knew the individual quite well. Their assessments were unexpectedly lukewarm. When I pressed for specifics, three of the four people I contacted explained that his main liability was the extremely high value he placed on his own opinions and his almost complete unwillingness to listen seriously to other views! As one said: "He's a my way or the highway type." How could this be? I could only conclude that his great, polished answer was a complete fabrication or, if true, it was the only such example in his entire work experience.

Although some organizations seek to quantify the interview scoring, there's no pat formula here. You will have to go with your gut, your intuition. You need to understand the attributes and talents you believe are most important for the particular job. Does the job require a self-starter, someone who has his or her own engine? Does the job put a premium on the ability to reach win-win compromises? How important is prior experience for the job in question? In general, I would look more to talent than to lots and lots of experience, but clearly there are some minimum experience thresholds for many jobs.

In the end, you must listen hard to what's said and what's not said and come to your best judgment. No one bats 100% in this important area. You'll make some mistakes. It's important to avoid making major ones. This uncertainty explains why many hiring managers tend to choose those they know. Some may see this a "good old boy network," but human nature is at work here and many people consider these closer-to-home choices safer and less risky. Of course, if this risk adverse philosophy prevents managers from choosing quality external candidates, eventually these outsiders, with their diverse DNA, will stop trying and that's not good for your program.

Developing Them

Most importantly, you need to make sure your people know their development is really up to them. They can't adopt a passive approach and expect you and the organization to ensure their progress and development. Your role, as their leader, is to encourage an on-going dialog, not just about their current job performance, but also about their future goals. In these discussions, you offer them your best counsel. You need to be honest about where you see their strengths and where you see areas where they should improve. You need to be authentic and not seek to avoid a difficult conversation by masking or swallowing your concerns.

In these heart-to-heart conversations, you will discover that many of your people are quite different from you. Believe it or not, most do not have the ambition to be the CEO of a Fortune 500 Company! At a minimum, you need to understand the individual aspirations of all your direct reports, your leadership team, and you need to appreciate their individual constraints. For example, one constraint could be a reluctance to relocate out of state or maybe just an unwillingness to move before the youngest child graduates from high school in three years. Career development suggestions also depend on individual preferences. Some of your people will place a high value on formal training while others see rotation to different jobs as a preferred way to learn and grow. It's not one size fits all so be flexible.

In the next chapter, I will discuss in some detail the open program culture that's essential to your program's success. To me, exposure to this culture, and an appreciation of how leaders at all levels on the team create it, is the most powerful way to develop your people (It's also key to attracting and keeping great people). As the program leader, you need to be a pragmatic optimist and recognize the attitudes and values you display are highly contagious. It may seem trite but you must *set the example* and be seen as authentic, with your actions always totally consistent with your words. Hypocrisy is the most deadly sin for a leader.

To develop your people, you must truly empower them. The best boss I ever had, on several occasions during the first few months I worked for him, decided not to approve, or even concur, with the recommendations I brought forward to him. Instead, he said: "You are the program manager and it's totally your call." Amazing! He was telling me he had confidence in my judgment and, although unstated, he was also saying he was willing to accept the risk of an occasional mistake.

If you are not actively pushing decisions downward onto your team and, instead, make all the decisions that are brought to you, you are in fact sucking decision-making up to your level and not empowering your people. Your team will see your concurrence and approval as validation that these many, small issues are above their level and require your active, and time-consuming, continuous engagement.

This is not the behavior you want. You want to develop people who do not continuously ask your permission but who, instead, make decisions appropriate to the information available at their level on the team. Of course, this means you need to trust them and rely on their judgment while understanding that, like all of us, they will occasionally make mistakes and seek your forgiveness.

When your people make honest mistakes, they are counting on you to support them. If they see you as someone who is overly ambitious and unwilling to sacrifice some luster to protect their backsides, they will not feel empowered. Rather, they will become overly cautious, passive types who will hurt the productivity and velocity of your team. And they will not develop.

Keeping Them

There is a real tension here. You need to retain enough quality people to have your program succeed, but you also need to let them go elsewhere when the individual's growth needs or the needs of the larger enterprise must be met. Unfortunately, some program managers operate as if their programs are their personal fiefdoms, with their teammates serving as vassals pledged to support the local lord (Program Manager) for life. You need to avoid this selfish mentality.

Once, I saw a very talented young man quit the company because the Program Manager poisoned all the internal, off-program opportunities for him. This Program Manager, at one point, even told him that if he took an excellent two-year rotation job he had been offered in our Washington, D.C. office, that the Program Manager would view this "disloyal" act with extreme prejudice and would ensure he did not get a good job when he rotated back. As a result, the individual quit the company and went to work for a small entrepreneurial outfit nearby. The enterprise lost his talent and experience forever. Even worse, within the following six months, another five very talented people quit the Program Manager's program, recruited by their respected and recently departed colleague.

This extremely personal view of loyalty is something you should avoid. Besides losing talent as described in the example above, this Program Manager put such a premium on personal loyalty that his team was peppered with mediocre people whose most singular quality was complete loyalty to "the man." Over time, program performance eroded in this corrosive and unfair environment.

Again, a key to *keeping* them, as well as a*ttracting* and *developing* them, is to create an open program culture where people feel trusted and empowered, where they feel they are being developed, and where the reasons they were attracted to work on your program in the first place are constantly reaffirmed.

CHAPTER FOUR: ESTABLISH AN OPEN PROGRAM CULTURE BASED ON TRUST

Besides all the science of program management, all the systems for defining and measuring and managing the cost, schedule, technical baselines, there are other arts you need to embrace to lead your program to success. The fundamentals are absolutely necessary, but they are not sufficient.

Creating a Vision, defining a Roadmap, and attracting, developing, and keeping talented people have been briefly addressed in the preceding chapters. In discussing the significance of your people, I described the importance of a program's culture since creating the right program environment is so critical to ensuring you have the right people on your team. In this chapter, I'll offer some more thoughts on the absolute need for an open program culture based on trust.

As the Program Manager, you need to recognize that you are the most influential shaper of the program culture. Your attitude and your example are the most contagious. If you are optimistic, your team is much more likely to be optimistic. If you are cynical, they are quite likely to follow suit. If you are open and straightforward, your team will follow your example, while if you are secretive and mysterious, you can expect to see that destructive behavior on the team. Because everyone is listening to and watching you, it's very important that your words and actions match. Your people will see any disconnect immediately and the hypocrisy will be obvious.

What are the features of the culture you need? A helpful exercise here is to remember the attributes of your worst boss. For some reason, this is usually an easier approach than asking people to recall the qualities of their best boss. Maybe the pain inflicted by a bad boss makes their lessons more vivid and easier to remember? The exercise will clearly define what kind of leader you don't want to be, and by extension, what kind of program leader you seek to be and what kind of culture you want to create.

The common themes that emerge are that people with a bad boss, and therefore working in a bad culture, do not feel valued, or trusted, or respected, or included, or treated fairly, or empowered. These people do not feel their honest opinions are listened to, much less adopted. Sometimes, a bad boss does not seek any other opinions since he or she has all the answers. Sometimes, the boss talks a good game but does not walk the talk. Sometimes, and this is hard to believe, people's opinions are solicited, but then ridiculed before they are dismissed. The result of this closed culture is a dysfunctional team that does not feel free to surface issues or share opinions.

Ultimately, many good people get discouraged and leave such teams. After awhile, sycophants, who spend much of their time trying to anticipate the likely opinions of the boss so they can simply mirror those prejudices back to him or her, can come to dominate the team composition.

So the culture you want should be open. Your people have to feel free to share bad news and share it in a timely way. No one likes unpleasant surprises. You don't, and neither does your boss. Real people (even senior people!) live in the real world and fully understand there will be problems and disappointments in even the best-managed programs. What's more important is how your program deals with these issues. If those problems are hidden or glossed over, your program will not handle them well.

On the topic of senior business leaders and their expectations, my advice is to never forget they too live in the real world. If your boss's boss runs into you somewhere and asks how your program is doing, take advantage of the opportunity to respond and don't just give him or her a smile and a thumbs up. They might believe all is well, but they are just as likely to think you are either dismissing their question as not sincere or that you really don't know your program well enough to give them a thoughtful top level answer. If asked, my recommendation is that you briefly outline one or two of your principal concerns and succinctly tell the big boss what you *and the team* are doing to address them.

You can't have a successful program with secrets since the team can't collectively solve problems they are simply not aware of. Your people need to be unafraid to raise their concerns and ask for help when needed. They need to be unafraid even if the issues they present are the results of their mistakes. At a minimum, this means not shooting the messengers. Even nicking them, or just firing into the air for effect, can discourage the openness you need. This does not mean you are completely tolerant of all mistakes. For instance, you can't accept the *same* mistakes or problems by the *same* team or individual repeated *over and over* again.

In collectively solving problems, you also need to drive a culture that has the discipline to systematically identify the (real) root cause of the problem and the (real) corrective actions. I add real in parentheses since some teams are tempted to kid themselves and avoid reality when the associated corrective actions are hard. It's often easier to just select a false root cause that has a simple, straightforward fix and doesn't rock the boat. Keep it real and don't let you and your team fall into this trap. Importantly, each corrective action must specify a completion date and identify an individual who knows and accepts that he or she is fully accountable. This corrective action plan must be documented and its status must be reviewed routinely until the actions are all closed.

As touched upon in the last chapter, you also need a culture in which leaders back their people and share accountability when mistakes are inevitably made. Obviously, there are limits here, but honest mistakes need to be accepted if you are to have an empowered, engaged team that has a passion for getting things done, and doing so with some urgency. Your program will never operate with efficiency and velocity if everyone on the team is seeking permission, concurrence, or approval from their immediate boss.

Earlier, I said that people should feel free to ask for help when it's needed. This is certainly true and removing obstacles that simply can't be removed by your direct reports and their teams is an important role for the Program Manager. Some organizations have institutionalized this commonsense and mandate that programs formally document the help they need from senior program or enterprise leadership. That's a fine practice, but here's a caution.

Some senior leaders ask their program teams over and over again if help is needed. If no help has been requested, these leaders remind their program teams they have not been asked. Some leaders pull on these requests because they genuinely want to help, which is good. However, other less sincere leaders, when there is the inevitable program performance issue, just wash their hands of any responsibility and hang it all on the program since they were *never formally asked to help*. These careerists often try to avoid accountability by saying "it's a surprise to me…I was never asked for help." They seek to excuse themselves in this way even if they routinely reviewed the detailed program health metrics and even if no help they could have provided would have made the slightest difference.

So be careful about those senior bosses that want to hide behind the help needed unaccountability cloak. They know full well that you and your team are there to solve problems (after all, they have "empowered" you) and really don't expect or even want you to flood their desk with constant cries for help. They simply want to protect themselves from criticism. These "leaders" are out there so be careful.

The program culture you need must be based on trust. At the enterprise level, there is an interesting dynamic because of the legitimate desire of senior leaders to understand their programs. To that end, a costly system that involves significant internal reporting and storytelling is sometimes created. To avoid the occasional program performance surprise at the enterprise level, the cost of doing business for all programs across the enterprise is increased, guaranteeing a general loss of profitability and often, still missing the leading indicators of a major and quite unpleasant surprise. This internal reporting can easily become excessive.

If so, it reflects a lack of trust downwards and, of course, it is wasteful.

When there is a lack of trust in the people the enterprise selects to head their programs, this internal reporting can become onerous. When your team devotes too much of their time gathering data, packaging it in different formats for presentation at different levels and are generally consumed with internal story-telling, they are not spending enough time focused on program execution fundamentals. Often there is not enough time to listen to the voice of the customer either. If your organization thinks it's more important for you to attend an internal enterprise gathering at some posh resort at the expense of your missing a planned customer meeting, you likely have an internal focus problem.

I recommend you audit how much effort your program team devotes to preparing for and supporting all the up-channel reporting of your program's status (daily phone calls, web-based meetings with required charts, weekly written reports, weekly packages of mandated scorecard charts, monthly off-sites, internal audits etc). If you believe the effort is excessive, you need to have the courage to raise your concern to your boss and to higher levels.

Although relief from some of these statusing activities may not be what your boss wants to hear from you, you should provide this straight talk. Sometimes, it only takes one person to tell the "emperor" he or she has no clothes, or at least should wear a jacket! If you are unsuccessful in changing the larger enterprise culture, you should consider hiring extra administrative help so that your key program teammates are not bogged down performing routine internal reporting tasks.

As the Program Manager, you should also audit how much internal storytelling effort you are personally driving. I am not talking here about program performance meetings focused on program status, customer concerns, risks, issues, opportunities and problem solving. I am talking about other internal storytelling that might not be value added. How much of this meeting and reporting tempo are you driving within the program? Is it excessive? Could you do with less? You need to ask your team and yourself whether the internal meeting and reporting activity is value added or whether it simply reflects a lack of trust. If you look at your complete operating rhythm and only see a few forums for customer interaction, you probably have a problem.

Clearly, some internal storytelling is absolutely necessary since your people's need to feel included depends in part on sustained communication. In addition, some of this important communication can't be electronic. However, I'm convinced you'll find at least some of this internal statusing is unnecessary. If it's not clearly necessary, I recommend you cancel the activity and see if it's really missed.

Internal storytelling is expensive and, when it's excessive, it's just plain *muda*, a bureaucratic sludge. It diverts attention from real program performance issues and it's not valuable to the customer. You need to strike the right balance.

Again, I see a lack of trust as the key driver behind excessive internal storytelling. Trust is essential to any high-functioning team. As a side note, I have found almost all the people I have worked with over the years to be trustworthy. One reason is that I go into any work environment assuming that the people I work with deserve to be trusted, so I start by trusting them, and generally, they meet my expectation. My most serious trust issue was with my program's Chief Engineer on a major capture effort many years ago. He was a smart guy and usually, but not always, had good ideas. Unfortunately, one of his ideas was that his opinion was always the only right one. As a result, he would never accept an outcome that differed in the slightest from his strongly held view. However, at some point in the team discussion, perhaps tired of advocating his view, he would express his support for the team's consensus decision. Soon thereafter, it would become clear he had not accepted the decision at all and he would offer some twisted explanation as to how he had misunderstood what had actually been decided. He could not be trusted.

When I met with the Engineering VP to insist on the replacement of my Chief Engineer, I explained the issue like this: if I wanted the team to wear yellow shirts on Fridays and my Chief Engineer wanted them to wear green ones, it would take us many, many, wasteful hours to "compromise" on something so simple but we would finally agree that the entire team would wear blue shirts on Fridays. On the first Friday after the agreement, everyone would show up wearing blue shirts except for the Chief Engineer, who would be wearing his preferred green one—and not understanding or remembering that we had all agreed as a team to wear blue. He was unacceptable to me as a teammate and was moved elsewhere. There was simply no way to trust him.

You also want a culture or environment in which there's a shared appreciation of the Vision and the ability by most, if not all, of the team to paint a verbal picture of this destination. The team also needs to understand the course set in the Roadmap and how their commitment to specific actions and results in this month, this quarter and this year will help achieve near-term benchmarks and keep the team on course.

I also recommend, in collaboration with your team, that you identify four to six top team priorities each year. Some organizations flow down many goals to their programs, with program financial goals and functional process goals all commingled in a goals list that can easily grow to well over 50 elements. Treating all these objectives as if they are equally important can easily blur the necessary focus of your team. Again, I recommend you and your team take the time to identify the top priorities, and not more than about six. This focus is important. That's one reason this book has just six main chapters, each corresponding to a recommendation for you, the Program Manager. If this book presented you with over 50 equally important recommendations, it would not be especially useful.

If you are required to list and track many goals, maybe you can put some of them in separate, subordinate categories and perhaps show how achieving these sub-objectives contributes to reaching the overarching top six priority goals. In goal setting, you also need to make sure you are not setting the bar so high that no reasonable effort can clear the hurdle. Also, especially if you have many, many goals, you need to be sensitive to linkages and interdependencies that can make achieving some goals mutually exclusive with achieving others.

In an effort to meet the worthwhile goal of reducing the cost of doing business, you often see parts of the overall enterprise lean out their local costs by adopting practices that simply push, like toothpaste in a closed tube, the costs to other parts of the organization. Often, the new place where the still-required work gets done is less efficient and the overall cost to the enterprise is actually larger. Unfortunately, people sometimes get a lot of credit for meeting their narrow goals while the overall enterprise suffers. You need an enterprise process that appreciates these linkages and guards against the unintended consequences of not attending to the big picture.

If you take over an existing program, you need to quickly evaluate the culture and identify the gaps between the existing culture and the open program culture you need. If you're lucky, you'll inherit a culture that's mostly open and functional and any gaps will be small (there's always room for improvement), but maybe you'll encounter a very closed and dysfunctional culture.

I once took over an advanced hypersonic missile program that had been run for many years by "scientists" whose primary, almost exclusive, interest was the continuing perfection of the technical baseline. In fairness, much of this focus was due to the customer's preoccupation with the technical performance of the concept being developed. Not surprisingly, this dysfunctional program had experienced schedule delays and significant cost increases. Ultimately, the cost increases had severely strained the customer's budget, forcing the government to abandon one of the two concept developments it had been funding. Surprisingly, maybe perversely, because of the technical performance *potential* of our missile design concept and in spite of our many, many execution shortcomings, our company was selected to continue development of its concept.

In spite of our selection, the customer was justifiably concerned about whether the team could deliver on the design's potential within the allowable cost and schedule parameters. At this point, I was brought in as an experienced program manager with a track record of solid performance on other technology development programs. It did not take long for me to realize that none of the program management fundamentals were in place: no one could tell you where the program stood with regard to cost or schedule baselines (in fact, there were no baselines!); no one could describe the key program metrics, other than some technical ones; no one could describe the longer term Vision since there was none—and therefore, there was no Roadmap, since any course will get you to a destination no one has defined.

Of course, the leadership team could meet and discuss the latest technical glitch and alternative fixes for hours and hours. There was no passion for meeting commitments and absolutely no chance this program culture would deliver a project result that would meet the customer's cost and schedule expectations. Collectively, we had to create from whole cloth the open culture I have described above. It was painful but necessary.

As an interesting aside, there was another serious problem. I soon discovered the originator of our design concept, who was an "advisor" and no longer even a formal part of the program team, was acting as its hidden leader. He provided a parallel path of communication to the enterprise leadership, to the customer, and to the team, including our key industry partners. He sometimes made commitments on the team's behalf and sometimes even provided direction. I had several chats with the individual, trying to explain why his self-appointed roles were unhelpful and I attempted to steer him into a much more limited, program-internal, supporting role. Unfortunately, he could not change; in truth, he wanted to be the Program Manager. It was a mess and some eggs had to be broken and some egos bruised to clean it up, and they were.

In summary, you and your team need to work towards a program culture that:

- **Is open and candid**; Where people are not superficially congenial; Where people don't hide important information; Where people feel free to ask for help; Where people tell it like it is and know that their expression will not be dismissed without fair consideration.

- **Is passionate about meeting commitments**, to the customer, to the enterprise and to each other; Where people hate recovery plans since they mean a commitment was not met
- **Is supportive of people** and tolerant of the occasional, honest mistake; Where people know their leaders will not leave them hanging just to avoid some tarnish on their reputation.
- **Is fair**; Where there are no "favorites" who are held to a different performance standard than others; Where personal loyalty to the boss is not the most important attribute.
- **Is trustful of people**; Where your team is not mired in unnecessary, internally-focused storytelling.
- **Is aligned**; Where people understand and are committed to the Vision and the course charted by the Roadmap to get there.
- **Is focused on the customer** and customer satisfaction
- **Is committed to action**; Where people collaborate and feel accountable to get things done, ethically of course.

CHAPTER FIVE: ALWAYS BE ETHICAL

I don't have much to inform you on this important point other than to emphasize my conviction that ethical business behavior is fundamental to your business success over the long term. Beyond that important business result, behaving ethically is also just the right thing to do.

In previous chapters, I have already talked to a few things I would loosely include under the ethics umbrella. If you are not open and authentic with your team and your customers, it's hard to imagine you will succeed in nourishing an ethical program culture. If you don't back your people and share responsibility for their mistakes, it's hard to imagine your people will be honest and forthright enough to consistently make the right, ethical choices.

Behaving ethically in competitions where a great deal is at stake (e.g., achieving your Vision) and your team is convinced your competitors are not being ethical is a real challenge. However, you need to avoid any temptation to follow suit. In international competitions, where foreign laws and cultural norms can be different, it will be doubly difficult to always meet the "Mom test" (ask yourself what your Mom would think about a possible action), but you must.

Throughout the evaluation and selection process, the customer will appreciate and ultimately value the integrity they see in their contacts with you and all your teammates. They know full well they will be depending on the integrity of your team to honor your contract commitments and deliver on your promises if you are the winner. Your team's obvious integrity is a serious competitive advantage.

After a successful international fighter sale, I asked several senior customer officials why our military jet aircraft was selected. Instead of listing the outstanding combat capabilities of our fighter or its affordable price, they stated that they had more confidence in our commitment, based on past performance *and the integrity we exhibited throughout the competition*, to deliver on our promises than they had in our principal competitors. How powerful!

Achieving an ethical program culture depends directly on achieving an open one since the ethical issues you and your team will confront are often not straightforward. Different people will have different views and you need to be able to publicly air out these individual perspectives and achieve a shared understanding everyone can accept.

I once worked for a boss who candidly admitted to his team that he sometimes felt that his ethical standards might not be as high as they should be. He told us he was "sometimes a little too elastic." He encouraged all of us to "push back" if we were ever even a little uncomfortable with an ethical aspect of a decision. To me, this candor and willingness to put these issues on the table, was very refreshing.

It's important to stress that being ethical in your business practices does not mean you are soft or a pushover. You need to succeed in the real world where the competition is fierce. It's not T-Ball where trying hard is what counts. You and your team need to compete and win in a marketplace where there are no silver medals. Taking steroids to improve your baseball performance is unethical; trying your best to dislodge the baseball from the catcher's mitt and score from third base is not.

Again, the leader is the principal influence on program culture and you must lead by example. All of the nice words about integrity will mean less than nothing if you are not authentic and if you do not demonstrate and insist upon complete integrity everyday.

CHAPTER SIX: UNDERSTAND AND LEVERAGE THE LARGER ENTERPRISE

This chapter is aimed at program managers who lead programs that are part of a larger organization or enterprise.

First, you need to always remember that your priorities are the success of *your program* and the *people on your team*. Although some will argue with this point, I believe it is not your major concern, as you pursue the two priorities listed above, to worry about how your actions affect the larger enterprise. Since your program Vision is fully aligned with that of the larger enterprise, your program actions should be in general harmony. Just get 'er done, with honesty and integrity, and you will serve the larger enterprise very well.

In these larger enterprises, your program is not just competing in the external marketplace, but internally as well. Often, the internal competition is just as intense as the external one. You are competing in the truest sense with other programs for resources--people, priority, investment funding—that your program absolutely needs to stay on your Roadmap and deliver to your stakeholders. Allocations of these limited and scarce internal resources to your program will necessarily come at the expense of others, but that is not your worry. Your responsibility is to make the strongest, honest case on behalf of your program and to be determined, sometimes almost stubborn, in your efforts to secure the needed resources. Of course, you need to maintain good working relationships with your peers in the push and pull of these allocation competitions.

My experience is that as long as you are honest and authentic and not playing games in these discussions, you should be able to push very hard on behalf of your program without compromising key relationships. If you are seen as excessively willful and obdurate, you will lose credibility and not be serving your program very well. However, if you have to sacrifice some popularity points to secure the needed resources, so be it. Popularity is not your purpose after all and being superficially congenial is not very authentic. As I said in the Preface, this book is aimed at those who seek to accomplish something worthwhile with their leadership opportunity, not for those whose goal is to just get along, rock no boats, and advance their careers.

As a caution, you will sometimes encounter two-faced people who work outside the formal process with continuous end runs to the boss to make their resource case and secure commitments in private. Sadly, many bosses are also susceptible to this backroom dysfunction.

I also need to mention that in many organizational constructs there are natural, often intentional tensions that arise between programs and the functions that typically provide the people, processes and tools the programs depend upon for success. The resource allocation competition described above often takes place in the context of securing functional support. If your program is the flagship program for the entire enterprise, you will almost automatically enjoy strong support. Functional investment in improved processes and new tools will be tailored to your program needs and the functions will be very receptive to your requests for the best people.

However, if your program is not a top enterprise priority, you will need to fight very hard internally. You will need to be a compelling advocate for tools and processes that, if not unique, are at least tailored to serve your program needs. You will need to be emotionally resilient since there will be disappointments that will force you and your team to nonetheless find a way to succeed. Again, you might not win the "most congenial" award and, in the end, your boss might have to tell you to "shut up and color," but your first priority is to the *success of your program and your people.*

Sometimes, you may find your goals and those of the functions are at odds. For example, you likely will have a profitability goal for your program that encourages you to continuously push for lower and lower costs of doing business. On the other hand, functions may be graded based on achieving a "100% functional excellence" criterion that actually drives costs into your program. Perfection sounds nice and, in some cases. 100% may be the right goal, but often, pursuit of that extra 0.5% of functional goodness can dramatically escalate effort and cost. Pursuit of perfection can't be "at any cost." There has to be some pragmatic balance here.

Also, internal functions are sometimes very insulated from any serious pressure to reduce their costs. Unlike an external supplier, whose price is the result of serious negotiations, most often in a competitive environment, many internal functions are essentially sole source providers who get to set their own, largely uncontested cost performance targets. As you can imagine, these self-imposed targets are rarely challenging. Worse still, with no incentives to do better, they usually become self-fulfilling prophecies and are often just met. If they are exceeded, blaming another function or the program is par for the course. Unfortunately, there is typically little recognition for how padded those internal commitments are and how much profit the enterprise is leaving on the table. Again, you need to push hard on the costs of these internal functional suppliers. Maybe you can succeed in having your program's profit goal added as a top functional goal?

The larger enterprise can sometimes include a Washington D.C. (WDC) team. If the US government is your customer; if federal laws, regulations and policies affect your business success; or if you are selling internationally, this will certainly be true. If achieving your program Vision requires attention from your WDC team, you will need a Roadmap that includes a strategy and actions for securing that support.

Again, if yours is an enterprise flagship program, priority handling by your WDC team may not be too difficult. Even in this flagship situation, there will be challenges. Most WDC teams are necessarily staffed with former employees of the executive and legislative branches of our government. Rarely do they have business or technical backgrounds. As a result, they speak a different language. Worse still, many of them may have little real allegiance to your larger enterprise, and almost no particular attachment to the success of your program. Maintaining their relationships with and continued relevance to other Beltway players is often, although not always, Job #1 for your WDC teammates.

If your program is not an enterprise priority, you and your team will need to be even more persistent and innovative if you are to keep your program and its WDC advocacy needs on any burner, front or back. My recommendation is for you and your team to make frequent visits so that they see you and your program as actual human faces and not just voices over the telephone or something even more abstract. Never miss an opportunity to educate your senior WDC colleagues or executives in your program chain of command about your program's needs for WDC office support.

CHAPTER SEVEN: SOME FINAL THOUGHTS

The purpose of this small book is to give you, as a Program Manager, some practical advice on achieving success as a leader. It is not based on management theory and may not be politically correct either. Rather, it is derived from a quarter century of program management experience in the real world.

Although I am convinced this guidance will be helpful, you should be skeptical and, after devoting some time for examination and thought, only embrace what makes good sense to you. Also, please remember that this book only talks to what I call the art of program management. Much of that art has to do with the leadership skills that distinguish great managers from those that are merely competent. All the management science of defining, measuring and managing the program baselines is ignored in this short text, but if you ignore these fundamentals, you, your people, and your program will not succeed.

As I said at the outset, the six main recommendations are the six chapter titles:

- **DEFINE THE DESTINATION AND ALWAYS KEEP IT IN SIGHT**
- **DEVELOP A ROADMAP TO YOUR DESTINATION**
- **NEVER FORGET: IT'S ALL ABOUT YOUR PEOPLE**
- **ESTABLISH AN OPEN PROGRAM CULTURE BASED ON TRUST**
- **ALWAYS BE ETHICAL**
- **UNDERSTAND AND LEVERAGE THE LARGER ENTERPRISE**

Now, here are a few closing thoughts.

First, never treat your leadership position as an entitlement. It's not. It's a position of privilege and you need to treat each working day as an opportunity to earn that privilege.

Second, don't let your leadership position go to your head. Keep your ego under control. A sense of humor is important and your team needs to know you have one. It will add a little fun to the job, a real positive for the team. A self-deprecating sense of humor is also a plus. Obviously, there are possible pitfalls here since some people can find offense in even the most innocuous humor, so you need to be careful. However, a humorless workplace is unlikely to be very productive.

Don't let your leadership position convince you that you have, or even need to have, all the answers. The team has the answers and genuine collaboration is very important. Don't just pretend to listen while constantly nudging the team towards your preconceived solution. Eventually, the team will see through this duplicity. You will discourage good people and end up with a team of sycophants.

On the subject of sycophants, it is sad but true that some senior people enjoy and even cultivate these "yes men/women" by nourishing a "Friends of XXX" club. These club members are known by all to enjoy a special relationship with the boss and people often go out of their way not to get on their wrong side. I don't know what psychology drives this need to create a personality cult but it is not all that rare and it can be harmful for your program or the enterprise to shelter such special, protected individuals.

In my experience, some of these "Friends" are often not even competent. Sadly, they are frequently assigned responsibilities well above their capability, where they create mostly havoc. I have touched on this in earlier chapters with reminders not to play favorites and to be seen as fair to all, but it bears emphasizing here as an important leadership attribute.

Third, be authentic. Your personal example of authenticity will help build a team culture that keeps it real. This open, honest culture will energize and excite your team and help create a winning atmosphere.

Fourth, always remember your primary responsibility is the success of *your* program and *your* people. You and your team are directly accountable to ensure your program meets its commitments to your customers and to the enterprise. Although you are not directly accountable for the performance of the overall enterprise, you must still be an enterprise team player. When you take actions that support the larger enterprise at the expense of your program, you should seek a downward adjustment to your formal goals where appropriate. In my experience, although this relaxation rarely occurs, you can achieve, at a minimum, some senior level recognition that meeting your original goals is now a higher risk. Unfortunately, if you fail to overcome the higher risks you and your team have accepted and fall short, my experience is that some enterprise leaders will have selective amnesia.

You need to get over such disappointments and press ahead.

Fifth, you need to be emotionally resilient. Because your attitude as the leader is the most contagious, you need to make sure your mood is positive and forward looking. George Burns is reported to have said of acting: "Sincerity is everything. If you can fake that, you've got it made." Although I don't endorse faking sincerity, I do believe that if you find yourself very discouraged, you need to do some acting and fake some determination and optimism.

Sixth, you need to ceaselessly communicate and seek to continuously improve as a communicator. This doesn't mean that you have to be a great orator or that you spend all your time talking at the expense of listening. It does mean you need to speak and write with clarity and that when you make a decision at a team meeting you take the time to make sure everyone that leaves that meeting clearly knows exactly what was decided.

Finally, don't forget there's life beyond the program you have the privilege to lead. You need to take care of yourself and your family. Good luck!

ABOUT THE AUTHOR

After twenty years in the aerospace industry, Mr. Hoerter retired from The Boeing Company in 2007 as Vice President, F-15 Program.

Earlier in his career, he served in the US Air Force as a test pilot and as a legislative liaison in the Pentagon. He is married and now lives in California, where he consults and teaches part-time as an Industry Faculty member at USC's Viterbi School of Engineering.